Apparitions in
Suodžiai, Lithuania

(pronounced Swa-jay)

From 1969 to the Present

by Fr. John Burkus

Printed in the U.S.A. by
The 101 Foundation
P.O. Box 151
Asbury, NJ 08802-0151
www.101foundation.com

Phone (908) 689-8792
Fax: (908) 689-1957
email: 101@101foundation.com

1st Printing, June 2000 — 5000 copies

ISBN: 1-890137-43-X

Introduction

*A*fter appearing in the fields of the village of Janoniai, the parish of Skiemonys, the Holy Mother Mary, as She had promised to Roma Macvis in 1962 at Janoniai, appeared in Egypt on April 2, 1968. However, She did not forget Lithuania and Her children, who had gone astray because of the persecution of the Communist regime.

In 1969, Our Lady returned to Lithuania. This time, She appeared to Anele Staugaitis Matjosaitis, a state farm cooperative worker, in her house outside of Suodžiai village, parish of the Finding of the Holy Cross, Kudirkos Naumiestis, in the diocese of Vilkaviskis. The seer is the daughter of the brother of Bishop Justinas Staugaitis.

· →»» · ‹‹‹← ·

Table of Contents

About the Author

Father Jonas (John) Burkus was born on December 3, 1913 near Linkuva, Lithuania. His parents were farmers. After he graduated from college in Linkuva on June 1935, he entered the interdiocesan Seminary in Kaunas, Lithuania, which was part of the theology-philosophy University there. He graduated in June of 1940 and was ordained on June 16 by his ordinary Bishop in Christ the King Cathedral at Panevezys, the Bishop's seat city. The ordination occurred on the same day and hour that the Russians began their occupation of Lithuania. In fact, the Russian tanks rolled by on both sides of the Cathedral causing tremendous noise.

He worked in Lithuania for four years— first under Russian and later under German occupation. In 1944, his health deteriorated and he received a leave of absence. He then went to the diocesan sisters on the shore of the Baltic Sea. When the Russians were reentering the country, his ordinary Bishop advised him, along with some other young priests, to leave Lithuania for fear that all priests might be killed. Thus, many seminarians and young priests left Lithuania for Germany, since this was the only country that seemed to assure them safety from religious persecution.

While in a Lithuanian refugee camp in Germany, he gave religious instruction to the children and wrote several booklets which were published there. When there was no hope to return to Lithuania, he immigrated to the United

States. He worked in the diocese of Grand Rapids and then in the diocese of El Paso, Texas. During 26 years of parish work in the United States, Fr. Jonas found time to write only two books, which were published.

After a domestic accident in 1975, he was advised to retire. He moved to Hot Springs, Arkansas, where there was a Lithuanian community. During his retirement, he wrote 18 books and several booklets on religion.

In 1990, Lithuania regained its independence. Since Fr. Jonas books were published mainly in Lithuania, he is a well-known and popular author there.

Apparitions in Suodžiai, Lithuania has been translated into Polish, Russian, Spanish, and now English. After 50 years of occupation and severe religious persecution in Lithuania, Fr. Jonas' books have inspired many souls to conversion.

Foreword

*H*oly Mother Mary, who had appeared in 1608 in Siluva, returned the Roman Catholic faith to the Lithuanian people when Lutherans and Calvinists were forcing the Lithuanians to renounce their Roman Catholic beliefs, and Lithuania was on the verge of becoming a Protestant country. Through the apparition of the Holy Mother Mary in Siluva and Her intercession, the Roman Catholic religion returned to Lithuania, while the neighboring countries to the north and west remained Protestant.

In 1940, Russian Communists occupied Lithuania. They wanted to destroy Lithuania's patriotism, and especially their Roman Catholic beliefs. Heaven did not forget Lithuania's tears, sufferings, and prayers. Through the prayers and sacrifices of the Lithuanians and of the whole world, Jesus Christ and His Mother Mary appeared at several locations in Lithuania. Most of the apparitions, which took place in Lithuania during its Communist occupation, have been forgotten. Only the local people in those locations commemorate them on the anniversary of their occurrences.

A completely different incident took place in Suodžiai, in the Diocese of Vilkaviskis, the parish of Kudirkos Naumiestis. Mystical signs there were instrumental in the rebirth of Lithuanian religion and patriotism, when in 1982, through the seer Mrs. Anele Matjosaitis, the Blessed Virgin Mary promised freedom and independence to Lithuania, eight years before the collapse of the Soviet Union.

This systematized book has been prepared from booklets and letters received from Lithuania, and is being reprinted from a Lithuanian book titled *Apparitions in Europe and America,* which is in its second edition in Lithuania. At a later date, a more in-depth book regarding the mystical signs in Suodžiai and their meanings for Lithuania and the Church will be written.

Many thanks to Jurate Bukauskas for translating this material and to Jim Lockwood for verifying the translation. Thanks to the publisher and the readers. It is my hope that it will bring good fruit.

–Fr. John Burkus

· ⇢≫⟩⟩ · ⟨⟨⟨⟵ ·

Chapter One

Anele Matjosaitis

The seer, Anele Matjosaitis, narrates the following about her life and apparitions: "I was born in Uzpjauniai village, in the parish of Kudirkos Naumiestis. From my youth, I had a hard life. It was especially difficult when I lived with my uncle. I had to take care of the animals and do other farm labor. I stayed with my uncle until I was thirteen years old. As I grew older, I stayed with another uncle here, where I now reside. I went to my First Confession and received the sacrament of First Communion at the age of ten, in my own parish church.

"I attended grammar school at Uzpjauniai. Often, I felt God's love and the desire to pray. During those times, I hid myself from other people, so that they would not laugh at me... I liked songs and sang often, but I was shy. I disliked bad words and acts... When I reached the fourth grade, I was unable to study further because I did not have the desire for it. Because of this, I did not finish grammar school.

"I had a great desire to go to church and pray. Once a month, I went to Confession and received Holy Communion... To attend Mass and Confession, I rode fifteen kilometers on a bicycle to the parish church at Kudirkos Naumiestis.

"In 1941, before the final occupation of Russia," Anele continued, "the German tempest of war found us in the village of Uzpjauniai. We had to hide ourselves behind a storehouse. Then, immediately after we had moved to another location, the storehouse was hit by a rocket. The structure was completely destroyed.

"The Germans came and instructed me to show them the farm buildings. They were searching for hidden Russian soldiers. They searched to no effect. I was with them and saw nothing.

"Years later, perhaps in 1970, I heard a voice: 'Do you remember when the Germans were searching for Russian soldiers? Know that they were there. If the Germans had found them, there would have been shots fired, and you would have been killed. However, you were needed for these times. Thus, I hid them from the German eyes and yours. They did not see each other...'

"When I grew to be a woman, I became acquainted with a neighbor who lived a distance from me, Mr. Pranas Matjosaitis," Anele related further. "We fell in love and, on May 23, 1955, we got married at the parish church. I was then 28 years old." (This would make her date of birth 1927.)

"My husband and I lived peacefully, nicely. He did not like to drink, and he tried to help everyone. He worked in construction," Anele added. "He listened to me, was peaceful and good. I loved my husband very much. On the day after our wedding, he told me that he would die soon and that he did not want to leave me with children, because it would be very difficult for me. Thus, we did not have any children.

"Things happened as he had told me. We were married for only a year and a half when he came down with a cold. This turned into pneumonia and, within a day and a half, he died. He was a religious and pious man. Towards the end, he would not let anyone remove a prayerbook from his hands. On his deathbed, he asked everyone's forgiveness, including mine, with tears in his eyes... I believe that his soul has left purgatory.

"After my Pranas' death, I prayed very hard," Anele continued. "I did not pray to Our Lord and Our Lady, because I did not have the courage to do so. Instead, I prayed to St. Anthony, so that he would give me at least a minuscule part of Jesus' love. With that, I knew it would be much easier for me to bear all life's hardships, pains, and troubles."

Chapter Two

Apparitions and Revelations

$\mathcal{A}$fter the death of her husband, Anele became reclusive. She prayed often during the day and night, asking for God's love and that His Will be done. At that time, she lived with an aunt who interfered with her prayers. The aunt taunted, laughed at her, and insulted her. After four months of such devout prayer life, she heard an inner voice say: "Your prayers have been heard."

In the fall of 1964 at around 11:00 p.m., while Anele was sleeping, she felt a hand on her shoulder and heard a voice say: "Wake up, do not sleep." After awhile, she began to doze off. Again, she heard the same voice: "Wake up, do not sleep." After the third time this happened, the voice continued, "Listen now." Then, she heard three knocks on the window pane and a voice said: "Know that Jesus Christ came to you and called for you to stay awake. Now you may lie down and fall asleep." Her aunt, who was sleeping in the bed next to hers, did not see or hear anything.

One evening, at the end of October, 1969, a light flickered in the sky and came down in Anele's yard. She had never seen a light like that before. Inside the light, she saw a dove. A light radiated to all sides from this dove and it appeared to be transparent. Its wings were spread wide, but did not move. The dove seemed to hang in mid-air. Startled, Anele cried out: "Lord, what is happening here?!" After several seconds, the dove rose in the air without moving its wings, and disappeared from her view.

Anele later said of the incident, "Neither the light of the dove, nor it's shining were similar to the light of the sun."

Anele believes that the dove was the Holy Spirit because, since that moment, she felt tremendous love for God. She took a Crucifix into her hands and could not put it away for a very long time. She felt completely different—she was no longer afraid to suffer or die for Jesus Christ.

She bought herself a small Crucifix which she could wear around her neck. She kept this Crucifix hidden under her clothing because she feared the Communists would try to take it away from her, or mock her or, even worse, mock Jesus Himself.

A number of years after her husband's death, Anele's aunt became very ill and needed much care. One evening, Anele was resting by the bedside of her aunt in a darkened room. The door to the house was locked. Anele relates the following incident: "Suddenly there was a light in the doorway and Jesus appeared. He wore a white tunic and a red mantle. The clothing was long and touched the floor. His long hair covered both shoulders. He had a small beard, thin lips, and a pointed nose. His eyes were deep and piercing. His face was extraordinarily beautiful and pleasant, God-like, attractive...

"He entered without opening the door. As He neared me, He did not take steps, but seemed to float through the air. When He reached the bed, He smiled slightly at me and said: 'You have great difficulty with this patient, but attend to her with love and respect. Whatever you do to her, you do unto Me. I will grant you many blessings. You will not have a long time to suffer with her. Soon, I will take her.' After saying that, He disappeared.

"Again, my aunt did not see or hear anything. My aunt lingered for another three months, and then died."

While walking through the yard in the evening of November 11, 1969, Anele heard a voice: "At 11:30 in the evening of November 14, Jesus Christ will visit you."

On November 14, Anele was trying to find *The Voice of the Vatican* on the radio when suddenly, from behind, she heard a pleasant voice say: "I have come to you as you were told."

Turning around, she beheld Jesus, standing on the spot where later, flowers and candles would be placed.

"He had long hair. His clothing was darker than the last time He appeared. A light, which radiated from His eyes, was so bright, it was difficult to look into them. His beard was small. His face was solemn, but full of love.

"On His chest, through His clothing, I could see the Heart of Jesus Christ. The rays of light, which radiated from His Heart, were so bright that they lit up the whole room. He held His right hand down with His palm facing outward, and with His left hand, He pointed to His Heart. I saw a wound on His palm. He said: 'I come because of the love I possess for the salvation of men's souls.'

"He told me to place flowers and candles on the spot where He appeared. He explained: 'When a priest brings the most Holy Sacrament, you light a candle. Therefore, let candles burn on this spot.' Then, He disappeared."

During the apparition, which lasted only a few minutes, Anele was in a state of ecstasy and was unable to move or utter a word. She did not tell anyone about this apparition.

On November 19, 1969, at 11:30 p.m., Jesus again appeared on the same spot. His outward appearance remained the same as on November 14, except that no rays radiated from His Heart.

He said: "Do not be afraid of anything. Be brave. Do not destroy your small altar with your own hands. If they want to destroy it themselves (the Godless Communists), let them do it. But most importantly, do not renounce Me. Pray for those who have gone astray so that they will return to God." Jesus stayed a while longer than the previous time, and then He disappeared.

Above is a painting depicting Christ as He appeared to Anele on November 14, 1969.

Anele's Godson, Rimutis, was visiting her at the time of this apparition. He did not see Jesus nor witness any strange light, but knew that something had happened to Anele. When he questioned her, she described to him the mystical events which had just occured. She told him not to tell anyone but, when he went to school, he told all his friends.

When Anele heard what he had done, she scolded him. Suddenly, she heard an inner voice, belonging to Jesus, say to her: "I come not only for you. I come for everyone. Why are you scolding this child?"

On November 24, 1969, at 11:00 p.m., there were about fourteen people visiting Anele. After they had prayed the Rosary, Anele began to read to them from the book *The Life of St. John Bosco*. Anele suddenly stopped reading and raised her eyes. She saw a beautiful Girl, about 16 to 18 years old. She stood on the same spot where Jesus had appeared. She wore a white dress tied with a blue sash. On Her head was a white veil. Her hands were lowered downward and slightly spread to the sides. She said: "My Son has stood on this spot twice. I can stand here also. Pray, pray, pray! Especially pray the Rosary for the people that have gone astray so that they will become better. Know that here was Mary."

Having said those words, with rays of light radiating from Her in all directions, She vanished. She had stood there only long enough to speak those words.

None of the guests had seen or heard anything, but they were concerned about Anele. They asked her what was wrong. She told them that Our Lady had just appeared to her. She also told them of her previous visions of Jesus. After this, the news of the apparitions spread quickly, as people widely discussed these events. The government also took notice.

· →≫≫ ·· ≪≪← ·

Above is a painting depicting Mary as She appeared to Anele, on November 24, 1969.

Chapter Three

People Visit the Apparition Site

O n order to go to the village of Suodžiai, located between Sintautai and Kudirkos Naumiestis, one had to turn west at Keturnaujiena using a very bumpy road, which at the worst of times was not passable. (It has since been improved.)

As word spread about the apparitions of Jesus and Mary to the widow Matjosaitis, people came to the site to pray. Fearing that they would be unable to get out of the ruts, people would leave their cars by the roadside to travel by foot through the fields to the farm settlement outside the village of Suodžiai. There, surrounded by poplar and aspen trees, stood the old buildings of Pranas Matjosaitis.

The visitors came to listen to Anele's account of the apparitions. They would record Anele's words in writing, because Anele herself could not. However, for fear of severe persecution from the Communist government, they did not leave their names. Therefore, it was very difficult to compile the records.

Anele received her new guests with a sincere smile, as if they were her closest relatives. If the visiting groups were small, she was able to offer a strong handshake to the men and kisses for the women. This made everyone feel warm and comfortable. After becoming acquainted, she would sometimes sit with them for awhile on a bench in the yard. Other times, she invited them inside her house immediately.

In spite of all this attention, Anele's personality did not change. She has always been a plain state farm worker who toiled at the cooperative. (During the Russian occupation, the land was taken away from the owners and made into farm cooperatives.)

There is nothing special about Anele's appearance. She would not be considered outwardly beautiful, but her eyes are deeply penetrating, her movements are purposeful, determined, and her voice is strong. Her hands are those of a farm worker who welcomes any type of work. Her heart is brave. She fearlessly talks about God's love, even to nonbelievers, and answers all questions sincerely, while keeping eye contact with all. She is without pride or arrogance. She is always pleasant and sincere.

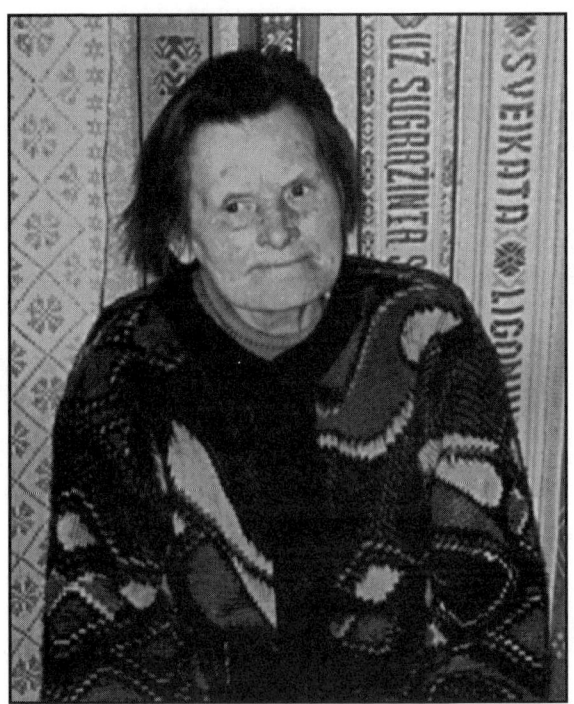

Anele Staugaitis Matjosaitis

The Matjosatis house was composed of two sections, with the entrance and antechamber in the middle. The part facing east was larger. By the door of the eastern part stood a large farm-style adobe stove. A distance farther stood a wardrobe cabinet and then a bed. In the corner was a table with chairs and by the window was a long bench. This is the usual layout of the homes of farmers in Lithuania.

Between the stove and the cabinet was a peculiar home altar, constructed on the location where Jesus and Mary first appeared in 1969, and then again on other occasions. Above the altar was a beautifully embroidered canopy, similar

The House in which Jesus appeared to Anele on November 14, 1969. He appeared on the right side of the house, which faces east.

in style to those that once hung above the Tabernacles in many Catholic churches.

In front of the altar, as in front of a Tabernacle, burned a red electric light similar to a red rose blossom. A dark purple carpet hung on the wall. On it shined the words, embroidered by hand and illuminated by light: "Jesus, Mary, I love You, save souls." This is a very powerful prayer, because it speaks about our love for Jesus and Mary. This prayer was taught by Jesus to Sr. Consolata Betrone, who died in 1946. Jesus also told Sr. Consolata: "One act of love is worth more than all other prayers."

In the middle of the altar stood a Crucifix, which Jesus Himself blessed when He told the seer: "I give this Crucifix such great power as if I Myself were nailed to it. I will forgive anyone who asks for My forgiveness while in front of it."

After this, many who prayed in front of this Crucifix have been healed and have returned to God, because God always keeps his promises (cf. Ps 105:42).

On the left side of the altar stood a statue of Jesus Christ. His heart is open and His hand is raised, as if He were blessing the people. On the right side stood a statue of Holy Mary. Her hands are lowered and slightly spread. On the left side of the wall hung a picture of the Sacred Heart of Jesus, while on the right side—a picture of the Immaculate Heart of Mary. On the floor lay a beautiful carpet containing a border of rue (the national Lithuanian flower). On the carpet were placed many candlesticks with burning candles, and various bouquets of flowers. The candles and flowers were offerings brought by people in order to show thanks, love, and homage for favors granted, or to supplicate to Jesus Christ and His Blessed Mother.

During the Russian occupation, Anele was not required to work on weekends at the state farm. On Sundays, many visitors would arrive after they had attended the Holy Mass at Kudirkos Naumiestis.

The people knelt and kissed the floor where Jesus and Mary had appeared, and prayed there for extended periods of time. Men, women, and even children prayed sincerely. When they arose from their prayers, Anele pleasantly asked them to sit with her and rest. She often asked them about their families, their lives, where they were from. She was sincerely interested in all of her guests.

She never talked much about herself but, upon request to do so, never refused, no matter who asked. Mostly, the visitors would ask her to tell of her visions and inner locutions.

A typical Lithuanian farm cooperative of the Soviet era.

Chapter Four

Interrogations and Threats

$\mathcal{T}$he Communist government and its officials followed with great interest the news of the apparitions of Jesus Christ and His Blessed Mother to Anele Staugaitis Matjosaitis of Suodžiai. They came from as far away as Vilnius, the capital of Lithuania, and told her that the altar and all it's decorations had to be dismantled. Since Jesus Himself had instructed Anele not to do any dismantling herself, she bravely told them: "I did not place any of the decorations there myself. The people placed them and I will not destroy them. I will not destroy the altar no matter what the consequences, even if I have to die for it."

When the officials wanted to dismantle the altar themselves, Anele told them, "Tear it apart and see what will happen to you!" As the men began to tear it down, they experienced a strange trembling.

Frightened and confused, they left the house and went to the yard, where the trembling left them. Upon reentering the house, they began to tremble again. And so it happened that they left without destroying the altar or its decorations.

The goverment did not give up, and many types of interrogations began. First, two officials were sent to question Anele. Soon after, five officials came and brought a physician to examine her. When it was determined that there was no physical problems, they took her to a psychiatric hospital at Ziegzdriai, near Kaunas. This is common practice in a Communist regime. They tried to make her insane. However, even the strongest "medicine" had no effect on Anele. Jesus Christ had told her earlier that she should not have any fear: "Drink the poison to the last drop. I will help you."

The physicians and psychiatrists, in their desperation, could only come up with the following diagnosis: "She is ill with an incurable disease." While Anele was in the hospital, Our Lady appeared to her to help strengthen her.

Unable to blame the apparitions on any real physical ailment, Anele was released in April, 1970 with strict instructions not to talk about "imagined matters and events."

When Anele refused to obey the government official's continued demands that she retract her stories about the apparitions, they tried threats, attacks, and even bribes, but were still unable to get the results they wanted. They offered to move her from her house and into a new house, which they promised would be nicer than the present one. Anele boldly told them: "I will not go anywhere from my house."

The Communists set fire to the roof of her house, which at that time was made of straw. About a square yard burned, and then the fire extinguished itself.

A bulldozer was sent to raze the house to the ground. While on his way, the driver saw the whole house engulfed in flames. He turned around and went back. In reality, he had seen only an illusion.

One morning in 1975, while Anele was hurrying to work, she noticed that a window of her home had been removed, and a metal tool was seen lying by it. A regional (district) official had tried to break into the house with the intention of destroying the altar and all the holy articles. When he removed the window, he envisioned a black casket inside. Frightened, he ran away leaving his tool behind. He related this later to his friends, while drinking at the local tavern.

Later, three officials arrived from Vilnius to get the matter straightened out. Upon entering the house, they too envisioned black caskets—this time there were three laid out by the altar. Frightened, they also left the house.

Soon after, a female official from Vilnius was sent, having told her comrades: "You men can't seem to get this matter straightened out with this woman. I will take care of this myself."

She was escorted by security to Anele's yard. Walking toward the house, she suddenly became paralyzed. Her comrades had to carry the "brave" woman back into her car, and all left in a great hurry.

One night, a group of assassins were sent to kill the seer. When they neared the house, they felt as if their feet were soaking wet. Upon inspection, they found that their shoes were filled with blood. Frightened, they left the premises at full speed through the fields. They ran so fast that one of the men lost his hat.

A meeting took place in Vilnius among high officials to decide what to do with this "disobedient person who was making fools of people with superstitions from the middle ages." As they began to discuss how to finally dispose of this matter, Anele entered the room through locked doors.

Looking them over angrily, she said, "How dare you discuss matters relating to me without my presence?" She then disappeared in a mysterious way. They became confused: "How could a simple farm worker upset them so?" (She had actually been nowhere near the meeting, and had never left her job on that day.)

The same thing occurred during a meeting of local state farm officials. In both instances, she "visited" the meetings by being in two places at the same time. Anele was unaware of these visits, so it would not be considered bi-location, because it is believed that those who bi-locate are aware of being in both places. Perhaps it was an angel, sent by God, warning the members of the meetings, in her name.

When the high officials of the meeting in Vilnius had calmed down after Anele's "visit," they began the process of strict measures, before something even more startling would occur to shake the public and even their own personal philosophies.

Ever obedient to Jesus and Mary, Anele did not cease talking about the apparitions, even after all the scare tactics and threats she had endured.

In 1984, Anele was given a written document —more correctly an ultimatum—that she move from her house and farmstead by September 1, to another place of residence. If she did not obey these instructions, the document said, her homestead would be completely destroyed, and she would be left homeless. Anele still refused, because God did not wish her to leave. From that time on, her visitors, both men and women, stood guard day and night in order to prevent someone from murdering her.

Chapter Five

The Seer and Satan

The interrogators and Communist officials were truly aided by the evil spirits in their many requests that Anele recant her visions, renounce Jesus Christ and His Holy Mother, and submit to their many requirements and instructions that nothing supernatural had occurred.

To prevent conversions, the evil spirits do not wish to have any real apparitions of Jesus Christ and the Heavenly Queen, along with Their teachings and warnings, be known to people who have lost their faith.

All true seers of Jesus Christ and His Holy Mother are often not only tempted by the evil spirits, they are often tormented to offend God and to renounce His teachings and warnings. Here are several examples from Anele's life.

Anele relates that, one autumn, "I had very strong temptations. It so happened that I could not even pray and did not feel any love for God. I could not even make the Sign of the Cross. The worst part of it was that I did not feel any love for God, as if a voice were telling me: 'What kind of life do you have? Is this your life? How can you live like this? Take a rope and hang yourself.'

"It seemed as though it would be so easy to hang myself, if only I had a rope. This went on for three days. I became extremely tired. I began calling for Jesus' and Mary's help and started making the Sign of the Cross.

"Suddenly I felt much better as if something had fallen off me. Again I felt God's love... I went to the antechamber... I opened the doors to the house. A storm had started and a piece of wood struck me in the head... I returned to the room bleeding because my head was cracked open, but I was so happy, because the evil spirit had left me, previously wanting to kill me."

Having told details of the apparitions of Jesus and Mary to her guests, Anele often added: "I will also relate to you about Satan. I have seen him also. I will tell you how it happened. My aunt was still alive, but she was very ill. One night, Jesus Christ said to me: 'Soon I will take her.' Then I realized that my aunt would soon die.

"Soon after, on another night, I looked and right there on the chair near the door, sat a cruel-looking man. I realized right away who he was. I said to him: 'What do you want here?'

"'I came to take her,' he said to me and nodded his head in my aunt's direction.

"'You will not get her, I say to you. Tomorrow we will bring a priest to her. Jesus Christ will take her.'

"'No,' he said, 'I will take her.'

"Then a great anger overcame me. I opened the door and told him: 'Outside!' He did not move. I went quickly to him. I did not feel any fear. It was very strange. 'Outside,' I said, 'and with speed!'

"Then, he fell down from the chair, shriveled up, somehow like a small child, like a three year old, and said: 'Don't do anything to me, I will leave by myself. Only, give me that choke cherry shrub that grows near the house.'

"I thought: 'What good is that choke cherry shrub? The person is important to me and not a choke cherry shrub... What difference would it make?' So, after a moment, I said to him, 'You can have that choke cherry shrub.' When I said that, he disappeared instantly. I did not even see where he went to."

On the following morning, Anele tried to convince her aunt into preparing for Confession, because the priest was coming. Her aunt became stubborn and stated that she did not need a priest at that time, and that when she became well, she would go to Confession. She kept talking in this vein while looking through the window.

Then, she said to Anele: "You better get rid of that child who is sitting in that choke cherry shrub. He looks so repellent and he is looking so loathsome at me. The whole time he is not taking his eyes away from me... He sits and stares at me, his eyes piercing me. He is so loathsome."

Anele realized then that the same devil was waiting for her aunt's death so that he could take her soul down to hell. This and Anele's constant prayers and faith helped her aunt go to Confession and receive the Holy Sacrament of Communion on that day. After that, the devil vanished. Her aunt died soon after, but she had made peace with God. The devil did not win her soul for hell.

Just before Christmas, perhaps in 1971, God woke Anele several times during the night so that she would be alert and pray because Satan was roaming the earth, gathering and carrying off souls to hell. She had trouble staying awake during that night.

One autumn day, Anele tried to dig a hole in the ground for storing potatoes during the winter months. A voice said to her: "Utter a curse and it will become easier. Curse at least once. Nothing will happen to you if you utter a curse once only. You will see how quickly you will dig that hole."

She looked around, but could not see anyone. The devil again said to her: "Curse and it will be easier. You work for everyone's sake. Serve me at least once."

Upon raising her head, she beheld a loathsome-looking man. He was totally black, terrible, having a red mouth. Anele said to him:

"I serve Jesus Christ and Mary. I will not serve you." When she mentioned the names of Jesus and Mary, he disappeared. Then she heard Jesus Christ within her: "You saw who was tempting you. Now you know."

· →»»· ·· «««· ·

~ *JMJ* ~

Chapter Six

Visions of the Dead

Since the beginning of the apparitions of Our Lord and Our Lady, the poor holy souls from purgatory have sometimes appeared to Anele. During their visits, she has talked with them, saw their sufferings, heard their lamentations, their calls for help. She has assisted them.

She had once seen her aunt, whom she had nursed for a long time and for whom she had prayed so hard for conversion. She appeared in a vision to her as having been saved, and said: "My dear child, I did not know how much I hampered you."

Once, while praying by the body of a dead person lying on a bier during a wake, Anele, kneeling by his feet, heard a voice: "Would you like to see how his soul looks?" She raised her eyes and saw that "his soul was gray like a shadow, like soil, but transparent. His whole soul from his head to his toes was full of wounds. It was so full of wounds that it seemed that there was not a single place that was healthy. Some of the wounds were deep, while others were shallower...

"He stood and looked sadly at his own body," Anele further related her story. "The soul looked somewhat different from a person, but very similar. If met, it would be very easy to say that this is the same person. I prayed for him. Then, after several years, the same soul appeared to me again. Now he no longer had so many wounds. He looked much cleaner. He told me, 'I did not know that you saw me right after my death, and that you saw how I looked. I have come again.' He asked me to pray further for the repose of his soul."

Another time, Anele heard a sound in the antechamber, as if someone from underground was calling her by name. She understood that a suffering soul was asking her for help. She immediately started praying for her.

Another day, Anele saw a man, covered with wounds, in her yard. She remembered having seen him in 1944, at the end of war—dead in a burned-out tank. At that time, she was 17-years-old. Now, after almost 30 years, she saw the same scene and heard the voice of his soul calling out to her by name. She prayed much and asked others to pray for him also. The soul looked like a person's silhouette, which had been soiled with dirty oil. Later, she saw the same soul, but now perfectly clean. The seer then knew that the soldier's soul was freed from purgatory.

While working outside one day, Anele saw a truck traveling down the road. Above the truck was a hovering soul. Later, she learned that the truck carried the body of a dead person from a hospital to its house, where it would be displayed for a wake before a funeral.

A voice awoke Anele from sleep late one evening. She quickly jumped from her bed and saw her body still lying there. A brightly-lit being took her to purgatory, where many souls faced atonement for each of their sins unatoned for while they were still alive on earth.

Her dead husband, in an apparition, asked her to pray for the soul of his friend. He needed only one Holy Mass before he could go to Heaven. She asked a priest to offer it, and then, her husband's friend reached Heaven.

"The Holy Mass is an amazing thing," related Anele. "Through the many graces received from the Mass, many souls are released from purgatory." On one occasion, for example, while attending Holy Mass, she saw that when the priest received Holy Communion, three souls, accompanied by their guardian angels, ascended into Heaven.

Chapter Seven

The Miracles of the Sun

Commemorating the anniversary of the first apparition of Jesus Christ, the miracle of the sun occurred in Suodžiai for several years on the 14th day of November. Several witnesses testified to these great miracles.

"On November 14, 1981, all who were present witnessed a miracle of the sun and were deeply affected," wrote a 60 year old man, who was visiting there.*

"When I arrived, the sky was overcast with leaden clouds. Then, about 11:35 a.m. Moscow time, the clouds separated and the sun appeared. Its color was matte. I could look at the sun with naked eyes. A colored circle formed around it,

---

*Nothing more is known about this 60-year-old man. Several witnesses, like him, would not give their names for fear of severe persecutions during the occupation years.

much larger than the sun itself. Then the circle started spinning around. The sun would began to tremble, jump around... Now, around the sun was a red circle. Next to it, in the sky, I saw the Blessed Virgin Mary with Baby Jesus in Her arms. It went on like that for about five minutes. The people fell to their knees in the mud and started praying loudly. The colored circles around the sun stained objects and people red, green, blue. After a half an hour, this was repeated twice more for a total of four times. The last time occurred at 3:30 p.m."

With tears in his eyes, the man continued: "From other pilgrims, I soon found out that not every one saw the Blessed Virgin Mary with the Baby Jesus. Some saw, in the sky next to the sun, Jesus carrying the Cross. Some saw Blessed Archbishop George Matulaitis. Still others—a black crown of thorns encircling the sun. Some saw a clock which showed not 11:35 a.m., but 9:35 a.m.—middle European time (the real time in Lithuania). Some saw a shaft of light across the house, on which shone the letters *INRI* (these are the letters placed above the crucified Christ, which mean: Jesus of Nazareth, King of the Jews). I did not see this, maybe because I had turned away from the house and was staring at the sun."

A man who had heard the narrative of the above-mentioned man, went to Suodžiai one Sunday in July, 1982 to interview Anele. When he arrived, he found about eighty people praying with the seer. He asked, "Did all the pilgrims on

November 14, 1981 see the miracle of the sun? Perhaps the nonbelievers did not see?"

"I believe that all saw," answered Anele. "Because when the miracle began, three civilian dressed men ran to the house, to the barn, to the shed, behind the shed, looking for someone who could be making something. However, when they didn't find anything, they returned to the yard."

Another question: "Were there some people who saw all the visions in the sky: the Blessed Virgin Mary with Baby Jesus, Christ carrying the Cross, Bl. Archbishop George Matulaitis, the crown of thorns in the sun, the clock, the letters on the house?"

Anele answered: "I saw everything that you said. There were other people there also who saw similarly as I did."

Then he asked of the people present: "Are there any people among you here now who were also present on November 14, 1981, and saw the miracle of the sun?" Three people replied that they were present and confirmed that they had seen the miracle of the sun on that day.

One of the visitors related the November 14, 1984, occurrence: "Glancing at the sky, I saw that the sun was a matte color and that you could look at it with the naked eyes. The whole sun was matte; only its edges shone brightly. It appeared that the sun was encircled with a bright ring.

Across the sky, originating at the sun, two colors stretched towards earth—violet and yellow—like wax... Then the sun started to tremble... After trembling for several minutes, it stopped. Later on, it trembled again. It started and then it stopped.

"The trembling of the sun lasted about twenty minutes with interruptions. I was shaken with shivers... And then, suddenly all was over."

Sr. Stase Burkus, a nun from Marijampole, visited Anele at Suodžiai and later, while she was in exile. Sister was a firm believer in the seer and the authenticity of the apparitions and messages. She sent the author of this booklet descriptive writings and drawings of the miracle of the sun which occurred on November 14, 1990. She writes about the miracle of the sun:

"On November 14, 1990, more than 3,000 people received Holy Communion there and most had also gone to Confession. At 11:00 a.m., the sun was bright, clear, and sunny. Above the sun, another sun could be seen in colors of a rainbow. Other colors were at both sides of the sun. Its rays went downward.

"Above both suns and lights, a wide light could be seen. The adjoining suns or lights sometimes dimmed, disappeared, and then reappeared. The light above, however, stayed constant for the duration.

While the priests were concelebrating Holy Mass in a tiny chapel, in which only the priests and their servers could enter, a large Cross appeared on the sun. Large rays radiated from the Cross in all directions. As the Holy Mass neared the end, the Cross and adjacent suns disappeared.

In the meantime, the second sun changed into something similar to a dove's wings, but without the dove itself.

"While the adjoining suns were visible, they emitted long rays. From the sun to the left there were fewer rays than from the one on the right. That sun emitted much, much more.

"At the conclusion of the Holy Mass, the second winged sun began to disappear. Then, all the participants of the Holy Mass recited aloud the Consecration Acts to the Sacred Heart of Jesus and the Immaculate Heart of Mary."

This description of the miracle of the sun as told by Sr. Stase might remind us of the Holy Trinity. The right-hand light means God the Father and His justice. The left-hand light reminds us of God the Son, from Whom we can obtain mercy through prayer. God the Holy Spirit

Pilgrims waiting on the confessional line, where every year since Lithuania regained it's independence, on November 14, priests hear Confession.

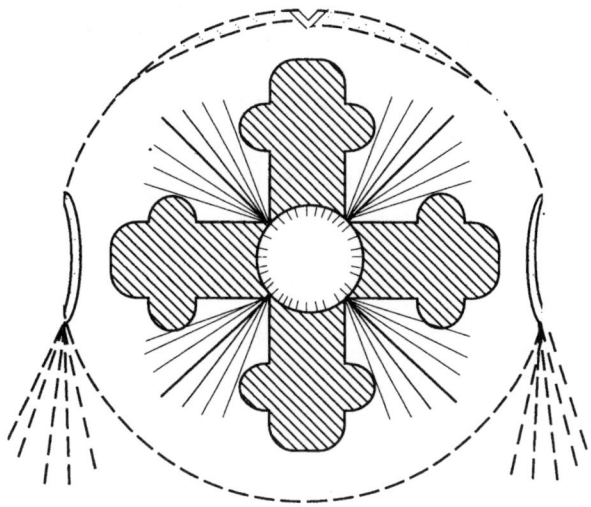

A depiction of one of the miracles of the sun as seen by Sr. Stase Burkus. This one occurred on November 14, 1990.

rules all creation. Through the visible Cross and our faith, we can be saved.

On November 14, 1994, for approximately a quarter of an hour, many people, perhaps ten thousand, witnessed an "unusual sun" with their own eyes. Some saw a second sun on the other side of the sun, and above it a large Cross.

It happens here that not everybody present see the same phenomena. In some cases, only the seer sees the vision. The ordinary of the Vilkaviskis diocese, Bishop Juozas Zemaitis, wrote: "People saw extraordinary phenomena, but not everyone related in the same manner." It is common for this to occur—some see less, others see more, and some do not see anything at all.

After the meaningful miracle of the sun occurred, Anele yet again reminded everyone and requested more prayers to the Holy Spirit. Very few people pray to the Holy Spirit.

· →>>> ·· <<<← ·

Chapter Eight

Healings

Many healings and conversions occured in the home of Anele Matjosaitis before its destruction. On both sides of the miraculous Crucifix on the house altar, many items were left, including pictures, crutches, and more, in thanksgiving for healings received.

On the left side of the Crucifix hung a large (approximately 32 in. x 20 in.) painting of Our Lady of Siluva. On the right side of the Crucifix is a painting of the same size depicting the Blessed Mother with the Infant Jesus. Both are very beautiful and expensive. The latter was a gift from a woman who lives in Palanga and who was afflicted with leg sores that would not heal for nine years. She came to the farmhouse to pray at the altar in front of the Crucifix. She prayed fervently for a long while and the pain in her leg abated considerably. By the time she returned home, she felt no pain at all. She removed the bandages from her leg and saw that it was free of ulcers and had healed without the benefit of a doctor or medication. She realized that the healing was the result of a miracle.

In 1974, she returned with the commissioned painting. She also left her crutches, without which she was unable to walk for nine years.

A baby girl was born with a disease. Her parents visited many doctors in Lithuania and in other countries as well. No one was able to help her. They brought the girl to Anele's home and prayed in front of the miraculous Crucifix. The child was cured. The parents returned often and in tears thanked God on the spot where Jesus Christ and His Mother Mary had appeared.

An elderly woman who was diagnosed as having a disease that had no known cure came with her family and was healed. In thanksgiving, they brought the beautiful large carpet which was laid down in front of the house altar, on the spot of the apparitions.

While taking their son to Kaunas for surgery to remove a large growth in his head, a family stopped in Suodžiai to pray by the miraculous Crucifix. Upon arrival in Kaunas, the doctors determined that the boy no longer had a tumor and was completely healthy. On the journey home from Kaunas, they returned to offer prayers of thanksgiving to God. The boy wrapped his arms around the Cross and cried with tears of joy.

Anele told of a family who brought their eighteen-month-old child to Suodžiai. The child was born twisted into a ball. The parents had consulted with the most prominent doctors, but none could help them.

Upon their arrival at the farm settlement, the parents placed the child in front of the home altar, before the Crucifix which Jesus Christ had given immense powers, and fervently asked for the Heavenly Mother's intercession for assistance. After returning home, they placed the child in bed. By morning, the child straightened out and was no longer crippled. The parents later returned to Suodžiai to offer prayers of thanksgiving for this miracle.

A woman by the name of Elena had a chronic inflammation of the pancreas since 1972. The doctors, unsure that she would live much longer, told her husband to make preparations for her funeral. After having been seriously ill for one year, she was close to death. A woman, who was in the same hospital ward, gave her Anele's address, saying: "Because of your strong faith in God, you should go and visit this holy place. You will surely be healed."

On August 17, 1973, the woman went to Confession and received Holy Communion. Her son took her to Suodžiai on the same day. Upon entering the room where the home altar stood, they fell to their knees and prayed as they neared the altar. While on her knees, the woman kissed the threshold, the floor, the spot of the apparition, and the standing Crucifix. She pressed the Crucifix to her chest and cried out loud as much as her heart would allow. She began to feel stronger and her pain faded. On her way home, while praying, she told her son, "If I am cured, then I will offer my whole first paycheck." She was cured. She did not suffer any more attacks. She returned to give her promised offering, but before she had a chance to give it to Anele, the seer said, "Please do not leave any money here."

Often, people offered donations to Anele, but she always seemed to know ahead of time what they were about to do. She always graciously refused. Perhaps her guardian angel informed her of who was about to leave money. Anele has never accepted any personal gifts, especially money. She did allow mementos for healings and conversions to be left at the altar, such as crutches, silver feet, amber hearts, etc.

During the Communist occupation, the doctors were unable to attest to miraculous cures, because they would have been severely punished. Now, however, it seems that the local physicians should feel a professional obligation to organize (as is done in Lourdes) and determine whether these people were miraculously cured at the altar in Suodžiai.

· →»» ·· ««←· ·

Chapter Nine

Conversions

At first, many priests and lay people did not show any interest or faith in the mystical signs which were occurring in Suodžiai. Due to the supression of events by the Communist government, they did not hear or read much about the events, healings, or conversions.

Fr. Peter, an exemplary priest and the pastor in Salos parish, held the events which occurred in Suodžiai as nothing more than gossip. In March of 1978, he was driving his car and got stuck in a snow bank. While digging and pushing his car, he became extremely tired and his heart almost stopped beating. He called out to the Heavenly Mother for help and suddenly he was given the strength he needed. Upon arrival home, he did not mention what had happened to anyone.

At Easter, a friend of Anele Matjosaitis arrived from Sakiai (about 156 miles from where he was). She told him that Anele had sent her with a message for him. She told him Anele knew he had almost died recently and that Holy Mary had heard his prayers and Jesus had saved him. Jesus told Anele to send this message, because the Blessed Mother loves him for the beautiful way he offers the Holy Mass. His prayers are pleasing to God. After this, Fr. Peter became a believer.

During early summer 1974, a man came to pray by the altar in front of the Crucifix, which Jesus Christ has given many graces. He kissed the floor where Jesus Christ and His Mother Mary had stood. His wife, however, would not believe. She questioned, "Why did not the Lord appear in a church to priests and devout people, and yet He appeared in a simple homestead to an agricultural worker who fed the farm pigs?"

In August of the same year, Anele went to Palanga, a resort town by the shore of the Baltic sea. The people questioned her about the apparitions. By chance, in the group of these people were the man and his doubting wife. The wife was so moved by Anele's testimony that she realized that God gives His graces to those who are worthy of them. They do not need to be educated or possess worldly beauty.

During an apparition to Anele, the Blessed Mother said: "Pray, pray, pray! Recite the Rosary for the fallen away people so that they would improve somewhat! Know that here was Mary."

Another time, the Holy Mother told Anele to let people know that one should not condemn another, because "someone might be praying for them, and they could be saved."

Having received these and similar instruction from the Holy Mother, Anele often told the people: "Because of this, many of my acquaintances and I pray and pray, arrange offerings of the Holy Mass, and offer our particular failures, adversities, and sufferings for the conversion of sinners, for the conversion of Russia, the postponement of the punishment, the postponement of the third world war, and for world peace."

In February, 1978, Jesus appeared to Anele and asked her to pray for the conversion of Russia. He told her that she should pray and make sacrifices even for the conversion of her enemies. Otherwise, it would be bad for the entire world. On that occasion, the Lord gave her this prayer:

"Most Sacred Heart of Jesus, be merciful to all. Forgive us our trespasses. Save us from the fires of hell. Lead our souls to Heaven."

One afternoon, around 3 p.m., Anele was in a great hurry to get home, because she had to go to work. In the yard, she found a woman with her daughter, who was about eighteen years old. The mother pleaded with Anele to relate something from her apparitions to her daughter, who was not a believer. Perhaps it would influence her. Because she was in a hurry to leave for work, Anele took her keys and wanted to lock the door to her house. Then, she heard a voice: "You can win a soul in just a few minutes, whereas a few minutes at work will not make any difference. Do not worry—narrate, and I will give her My grace. Pay close attention to the girl. When she starts to tremble, know that My grace has reached her." Anele invited them into the house.

When the girl saw the altar and the Crucifix on it, she said to her mother, in anger, "Mother, where have you brought me?"

"Here, in this place, Jesus Christ and His Mother Mary have appeared," her mother answered.

"Mother, you know that I do not believe. There is no God and He cannot exist."

When Anele began to tell her story, the girl quieted and listened. As the narrative continued, the girl became agitated and began to tremble. Soon she started to cry very hard and then said loudly, "I now believe that God is truly present!" All three embraced and cried because of the great mercy and goodness of God.

On another occasion, a twenty-year-old man came with the pilgrims. He was a nonbeliever. He came only to look around and perhaps make fun of it. While sitting in the corner of the room, he suddenly started to tremble and cry loudly. When others asked what had happened, he answered: "I now believe that there is God!" Going to another room, he told those listening that he saw his whole life flash before him, as if in a television film. He saw all his sins and what awaited him if he died then. "I will change my life now," he promised.

Anele noticed that one of her neighbors was always sad. In prayer, she asked God the reason for his sadness. An inner voice explained to her: "He keeps some sins hidden. Urge him to make a good Confession." After a long entreaty, he did go and have a full Confession. Later his joy was immense. He thanked Anele and, most of all, God.

· →》》 ·· 《《← ·

Chapter Ten

Ecstasies and Visions

During the apparitions of Jesus Christ and His Blessed Mother, Anele falls into ecstasy. She describes this event in the following manner:

"During an ecstasy, my body grows numb. I no longer feel my body. It is as if it separates from me. Only the spiritual world influences my soul. This has occurred during all of the apparitions of Our Lord and Our Lady. Each time, however, the experiences in my soul are different. I cannot describe the feelings with words."

In addition to visions of Jesus and Mary, several times, Anele has experienced visions of the Holy Spirit in the form of a dove or a tongue of flame. The first instance of a vision of the Holy Spirit has already been mentioned.

On the evening of May 10, 1975, Anele and several of her neighbors were saying the novena prayer to the Holy Spirit. While they were reciting the litany of the Blessed Virgin Mary, "a strong roaring noise was heard," Anele relates. "It sounded like an airplane or wind roaring and whistling... A large tongue of fire invaded the room. It went around the outer edges of the room in the air and disappeared by the table in the middle of the room. The other women, who were kneeling with me, did not hear any roar, nor see any light. During the vision, I did not feel my body and I do not know the length of the vision."

In 1984, on Holy Thursday, Anele "saw Jesus Christ praying in the Garden of Gethsemane. He knelt on the ground. His folded arms rested on the brim of a rock. Close by was a shrub similar to a lilac. Behind Him, in the distance, was a sparsely planted forest. The face of Jesus appeared tired and wet with perspiration. Droplets of blood seemed to seep from His face... Further away, by a rock, I saw the three sleeping apostles."

Anele described an apparition that occurred on Good Friday: "On Good Friday, I saw how Jesus Christ brought the Cross to Calvary. When the Cross was reassembled, the guards ripped the clothing, which had stuck to His wounds, from His body. His wounds reopened and He was in great pain. He lay down on the Cross without any aid and spread His arms out so that they could be nailed down.

"Further vision was broken off. Jesus explained that I would have been unable to handle the vision. He explained also that He was nailed to the Cross not through the palms of His hands, but through His wrists, although He is depicted as being nailed down through the palms. However, if the Lord gives someone the grace of His wounds and pain, the wounds and pain are usually in the palms because the wounds in the wrists would be unbearable.*

"On Good Saturday, Jesus Christ said to me: 'I departed for hells (Abraham's protection, where the righteous were awaiting their redemption).' He (Jesus Christ) was illuminated and holes were visible in His wrists," related Anele. Hearing this, a woman from the group asked Anele: "I have heard that you have physical pains from the wounds of Christ. Is that true?" Anele did not respond to the question, but simply said: "Pray for me, pray for me."

Anele said that once Jesus Christ appeared so severely beaten up and tortured that the vision was terrible to behold. Jesus said to her: "I suffer now more from the wickedness of the world than from the Way of the Cross."

· ->>>> ·· <<<<- ·

*Some mystics have their stigmata in the wrists. Examples of this are visionaries Gladys de Motta of Argentina, and Blessed Padre Pio.

Chapter Eleven

Destruction of the Farmstead

A judgment was issued by the courts stating that on June 26, 1985, the farmstead of Anele Matjosaitis would be destroyed.

The destruction was organized by Peter Jurksaitis, who was the president of that state farm, five militiamen and two men with bulldozers from Sakiai, the county seat, and ten workers from the farm,

The workers gathered as much furniture and as many pictures and clothes as they could into a truck and drove it two miles to the cooperative lodgment, where a room was assigned for Anele. Many things did not fit in the truck and were left behind in the yard.

With the use of the bulldozers, all the buildings in the farm settlement were destroyed. They pushed the debris in a pile and put a match to it. The buildings, farm equipment, and grains for feed and bread all burned together. Nobody even bothered to save the grain.

A group of people gathered and watched and cried. Even some of the militiamen were agitated by the destruction. Only the seer remained completely calm. She stood close by to the group of people and prayed the Rosary. Not a single tear fell on her face, although her heart was on fire— not for her worldly goods, but for the cruelty of men. Later, she said: "God gave me a lot of strength."

After the people who had destroyed and razed the homestead had left, the witnesses prayed on their knees to ask God's forgiveness for the atrocities committed there. They asked for mercy and forgiveness for those who had committed the crimes. They asked for their conversion and for their salvation.

After everything had almost completely burned and most had departed, Anele remained kneeling for a long time near the spot of the apparitions. She asked for God's mercy upon those who destroyed all this. She prayed to the Blessed Mother for intercession to God for those who needed His graces.

Anele knew she did not want to stay at the room assigned to her. So, being obedient to God's will, after finishing her prayers, she took a board from the flooring on which stood Jesus Christ and His Mother Mary. This board had not burned.

Although she was allowed to take much from her home, she left taking only her Rosary beads, her passport, and the flooring board, in accordance with words that Jesus Christ had told her: "You have a free will to choose either things or Me. Whatever you choose, I will not contradict you. If you choose Me—then do not agree to accept any goods; do not agree to the destruction of the homestead. If the agents of the government want to do something, allow them to do this, but without your agreement. I will take care of you." She left to go into the unknown, peacefully reciting the Rosary, with no other possessions, and not knowing where she would find a place to lay her head.

She eventually settled with some of her acquaintances in Kaunas, fifty five miles from the site of the original apparitions and her home. Later, she related: "I left in my simple work clothes, with sandals on my feet, with the simplest of sweaters, without taking a better sweater along."

Anele prays near the apparition site after the Communists burned her home.

The people who witnessed the destruction and fire of the settlement, recalled that the sight was terrible. Soon after, the trees surrounding the settlement were cut down and taken away. The furniture that was taken away to the cooperative lodgment, stood in the yard. The officials thought that Anele would come and retrieve them. Nobody came to take it. The Crucifix that had stood on the home altar was later found in a ditch a mile away from the site of the apparition.

In order to justify its nefarious works, the officers of the Communist party decided to build an airport on the site. In a letter dated November 27, 1995, ten years after the fire, this author received a letter from Bishop Juozas Zemaitis, the ordinary of Vilkaviskis Diocese, stating: "The president of the farm cooperative, Peter Jurksaitis, who had gone the day after the burning to look over the location for the airport, was pushing around the burned Crosses and Rosaries with his feet. While walking home through the fields, he fell down and died."

Two other men, who also took an active part in the destruction of Anele Matjusaitis' homestead, were called to God's judgment that same year—1985. One was a 20-year-old land surveyor, who had been measuring Anele's land and hammering stakes of wood in preparation for the construction of the airport. The other man was an enforcer of the judicial judgment. He was also the young man who, with the urging of Peter Jurksaitis, had earlier dug up all the beet roots from Anele's garden.

Anele prays regularly for all three men, requesting Masses for the repose of their souls. Perhaps one or all of them had the opportunity to say, "I am sorry that I have done this."

The airport, which was never utilized, was constructed between the late fall of 1985 and June 30, 1988. Pilgrims were forbidden to visit the site during the construction, and even for some time after. During this time, on the first Friday of every month, the people of faith gathered at the parish church of the Finding of the Holy Cross, in Kudirkos Naumestis. There they asked God's pardon for the sins of the people.

In September 1988, the faithful commemorated 2000 years since the birth of the Blessed Virgin Mary. During this celebration, the religious and patriotic movement for the rebirth of Lithuania began.

On November 14, 1988, at the site of the original apparitions, more than a thousand people gathered. They came to honor Jesus and Mary for the special graces granted to Lithuania and to obtain, by prayer, spiritual help, religious freedom for the Church, and independence for Lithuania.

In preparation for the celebration of the 20th anniversary of the first apparition, the local faithful people erected, with their own funds, a wooden carved pole. On it are depicted Jesus Christ, the Holy Spirit, and Mother Mary, with Her hands clasped in prayer.

As the Communist regime softened its stance, on February 16, 1989, for the first time since the occupation started in 1940, the Independence of Lithuania was celebrated publicly. The intolerance for God, Church, and the native land of Lithuania was less harsh as was the persecution of the pilgrims to the Suodžiai homestead, where the airport still lay unoccupied.

On the 20th anniversary of the first apparition, November 14, 1989, Holy Mass was celebrated there for the first time. The carved pole was placed near the altar. More than three thousand pilgrims attended the Mass. Many saw miraculous signs in the sky.

The local people at the wooden chapel in 1990 are seen carrying the miraculous Crucifix which was recovered from a ditch a mile from the unused airport.

Chapter Twelve

The Apparitions Continue

The apparitions of Our Lord and Our Lady, which began in 1969 at Suodžiai, still continue to this day. Here are several examples.

On November 24, 1992, at 2:00 a.m., an inner voice urged Anele to get up and go to the yard. Upon arriving at the yard, she saw a Woman dressed entirely in black. It was our Holy Mother. She gave Anele a little box and told her to fill it up with balsam, the supplication of pardon.

Two days later in the evening of November 26, 1992, the Holy Mother appeared again to Anele in her room. Her attire was gray and Her face was uncovered. She affirmed that it was She who had appeared two days earlier. She mentioned Yugoslavia where a civil war was raging. She stated that Her Son is especially offended with the following four sins: pornography, abortion, disregard of holy days, and the contempt of the Holy Sacraments.

She said that people do not pray or attend the Holy Mass enough. "There is not anything more important than the sacrifice of the Holy Mass," She added. "People have to ask God's mercy and pardon. There is a need for prayers and sacrifices so that the same does not occur here as is occurring in Yugoslavia." She then said, "Here (in Lithuania) the people are different and the situation is better, because it is possible to obtain God's mercy and forgiveness by prayer," (that Lithuania could hold out its independence). Holy Mother then disappeared.

In the fall of 1994, Anele related and a person known only as V. Kazlauskas from Kaunas transcribed the following account: "The Lithuanians from Canada had donated, as a gift, a cross having a pedestal. It was about 16 inches in height. Anele wanted to decorate it with a chip from the relic wood which had been removed from the burned out floor where the apparitions of Jesus Christ and the Holy Mother had occurred. Just as she began to whittle it off, her fingers started to burn strangely. Fear and uneasiness overtook her. Removing a chip of wood with a knife, she felt a deep love for Jesus Christ, and fell into ecstasy. She saw Jesus sitting at the table dressed in red clothing. He said to her: 'You were so moved, because My feet touched this floor. You were told (in 1982) that Lithuania would regain its independence through blood and tears. A big mistake is taking place when the West is imitated. That is the reason why My Mother is weeping. She is weeping in Lithuania only in tears. They are imitating the West where my Mother is already weeping tears of blood.

"'A time will come when even here (Lithuania), My Mother's tears will be of blood. We are nearing a time when the people here will receive Me (the Eucharistic Christ) in their hands. Only priests (and deacons) can touch Me with their hands. I died on the Cross out of love. Now, there is no love or esteem. My servants (bishops and priests) are doing Me a disservice by pushing the people to receive Me while standing up. The priests need a lot of prayers. Tell this to the people.'"

Anele gives an example of this lack of respect, which was also recorded by V. Kazlauskas. Anele relates:

"On September 13 in Siluva, on the anniversary of Our Lady's appearance there in 1608, I saw a great lack of respect for Christ in the Holy Eucharist. There were large crowds of pilgrims on that day. The church was completely full. Even the church-yard was packed with people. I saw how a priest was distributing the Holy Eucharist. The people were forcing their way to the priest, pushing each other, pushing the priest at the same time as they jostled with their elbows his hand, in which he held the Holy Eucharist... If the Holy Eucharist were given out to the kneeling people, there would not be such disorder... Returning home that same evening, I heard a familiar voice:

"'You saw what happened and you are still not saying anything. You have to speak out.'"

Anele added: "By receiving Christ with love, kneeling with respect, we will wipe the tears of the Holy Mother."

On the evening of September 6, 1997, during the night prayers of the First Friday/First Saturday vigil, many pilgrims, especially from Lower Lithuania, were gathered at the Chapel of the apparitions at the settlement of Suodžiai.

On that Friday evening, all were praying for the soul of the deceased Princess Diana of England. During these prayers, Princess Diana, who had been buried that morning, appeared to those gathered, and held tightly to a statue of the Blessed Virgin Mary. After about an hour, she left the statue, turned to the people, and spoke in Lithuanian, so that all could understand. She said, "I am very happy that I died before I committed adultery." She was very happy and thanked God and the Blessed Virgin Mary for being killed.

After these words, her soul was shown to the seer. Small stains were visible on it. By this, we understand that she performed her reparations of sins while still on earth. Therefore, she was saved.

Several moments after the words uttered by Diana, Anele felt and saw that on her right stood Mother Teresa of Calcutta. She explained the reason for her death, while no one at the chapel was aware that she had died.

She stated that because her physicians did not allow her to attend the funeral of Princess Diana, she was so bereaved that her heart could not sustain such sorrow and therefore stopped. Upon hearing this, several people went to the residence of Anele and found out that Mother Teresa had just died.

Chapter Thirteen

The Chapel on the Site of the Apparitions

During the occupation of Lithuania, Anele Matjosaitis saw an apparition of a beautiful church and large buildings that would stand on the spot where Jesus Christ and His Mother Mary has appeared in Suodžiai. She saw an image of this shrine eight years before Lithuania regained its independence.

After the razing of the homestead, the local people erected a small Crucifix and the women often brought flowers and candles. During the day, the atheists often would clear the proposed airport site of flowers, candles and Crucifixes. When that occurred, the people of faith would place a new Crucifix, flowers, and more candles. The original Crucifix which was blessed by Jesus was broken into pieces and thrown away into a ditch about a mile away from the apparition site. It was found a month later. The same fate awaited

A cross of flowers and candles are placed on the unused runway, before the chapel was built.

other Crucifixes erected on the site during the construction of the airport until even after it's completion on June 30, 1988.

When Lithuania regained its freedom and independence on March 11, 1990, "a small wooden chapel was built by the people using their own funds and initiative. It was completed by November 14," wrote bishop Juozas Zemaitis, MIC, in the previous mentioned letter dated November 27, 1995. "They erected it on the site where Jesus Christ and His Mother Mary first appeared in 1969."

The site itself was inside the chapel. It was adorned with two pictures above the altar. One was that of the radiating Sacred Heart of Jesus and the other was of the Virgin Mary with Her arms stretched out. Anele had seen this in a vision. Between these pictures, behind the altar stood the previously mentioned lower portion of the carved pole, and in front of it a Crucifix and candlesticks. A picture adorned each side of the shrine.

"When the Lithuanian Renewal Movement began," added Bishop Juozas Zemaitis, "a group of faithful people began organizing the construction of a new house for Anele Matjosaitis, whose original home had been destroyed in June, 1985."

Anele, standing in the chapel. Notice the carved pole behind the altar.

On January 28, 1990, shortly before Lithuania regained its independence, Jesus appeared to Anele in a church in Kaunas and said, "Do not leave Me alone in Keturnaujiena (a neighboring village of Suodžiai)." So, when the construction of her new house was completed, very close to the original apparition site, Anele returned from Kaunas. She returned from exile because she understood that it was the will of God and the Blessed Mother Mary that she spread the word of the apparitions, the teachings, and also to help bring the people to God and their salvation.

On November 14, 1990, Holy Mass was offered for the second time at the site of the apparitions by Msgr. Donatas Jasulaitis, the pastor of the Finding of the Cross of Kudirkos Naumiestis, and a newly ordained priest, who a few years previously, had found his vocation at the site of the apparition, the farmstead outside of Suodžiai.

The new chapel, still under contruction, in 1995.

Anele's new home. Pilgrims facing the chapel.

"In July, 1995, the construction of a larger chapel began, under the direction of the pastor of Kudirkos Naumiestis, Monsignor Donatas Jasulaitis, and financed by a family from Australia—Mr. & Mrs. Aras and their son. It is financially assisted by the local pilgrims who visit Suodžiai," wrote Bishop Juozas Zemaitis to the author.

"Perhaps we will be able to build and furnish it in three years," added the Bishop. "We are thinking of calling it the Chapel of Holy Mary, the Merciful. The chapel will be 4,290 square feet. I have allowed the priests to celebrate the Holy Mass on November 14, when large crowds of pilgrims gather. On that day we commemorate the first apparition of November 14, 1969. This year, 1995, over 4,000 received Holy Communion. I personally have not been present on these occasions, and have not yet celebrated Holy Mass there."

The new chapel, made of white bricks, has been constructed on the site of the apparition. The previous wooden structure, for some time, remained inside the new structure. so that the priests had an altar on which to celebrate Holy Mass. At other times, the pilgrims come to visit the site of the apparitions of Jesus Christ and His Holy Mother.

Chapter Fourteen

What Does the Church Say?

When the bishop ordinary of Vilkaviskis was questioned, he responded (in the above mentioned letter of 1995): "Until there are clear supernatural manifestations in Suodžiai, there will not be any commission established to investigate them."

A commission composed of physicians, theologians, psychiatrists and psychologists is the apparatus which is used to determine if a seer is psychologically healthy. Physicians determine whether the healed people truly had incurable illnesses and whether they are now truly cured. The theologians determine whether all the revelations are in accord with the Holy Bible, Tradition, and the teachings of the Catholic Church.

Normally, such commissions are formed while the seers of the apparitions are alive and the physicians and people who have been cured are capable of testifying to their conditions. Upon receiving the results of the investigation, the bishop ordinary then makes a decision as to the authenticity of the apparitions and revelations. He would reach his decision after conferring with the prefect of the Sacred Congregation for the Doctrine of Faith or other members of the Congregation. The decision of the local bishop ordinary is final.

Therefore, having such an important responsibility, he is very cautious, and is in no hurry to make a judgment on the authenticity of apparitions and mystical revelations. However, it is

Monsignor Donatas Jasulaitis, Anele's pastor and spiritual director, November 14, 1997.

possible to draw the following conclusions, based on the letter from bishop Juozas Zemaitis and other sources:

1) In the letter written on November 27, 1995, the bishop ordinary expressed himself to this author, that: "November 14 commemorates the anniversary of the first apparition which occurred on November 14, 1969." This acknowledges that an apparition did indeed occur in 1969 and by calling it the "first," he acknowledges that more followed.

2) The bishop gave permission for the construction of a chapel and allows Holy Mass to be celebrated by visiting priests on the day commemorating the first apparition. Therefore, he has allowed the cult of Our Lord and of Our Lady of Suodžiai, and indirectly, the apparitions and revelations which have been occurring in the settlement of Suodžiai since November 14, 1969.

Furthermore, the local bishop has not forbidden the propagation of revelations which Anele Matjosaitis has received and continues to receive, because they do not contradict the Holy Bible, Tradition, or the teachings of the Catholic Church. It is also apparent, that the crowds visiting the site of the apparitions of Jesus Christ and His Mother Mary are increasing in number year by year, conversions are occurring, and the faith of the visitors is strengthened.

It seems that all of the conclusions are favorable. They speak for the authenticity of the apparitions and revelations. However, we respectfully await the final decision of Our Holy Mother, the Church.

We are grateful for all of these happenings to Jesus Christ and His Blessed Mother, to the patron saints of Lithuania, Saint Casimer, and Blessed George Matulaitis, a son of Lithuania, who are very concerned about the salvation of all people, but especially those, in whose care the latter ones were given by Heaven. We give them thanks daily by conversion, prayer, repentance, sacrifice, and the dissemination of the revelations received in Suodžiai.

May these revelations continue to bring glory and honor to God in the highest and God's grace to people of good will.

The chapel in Suodziai, Luthania. The Stations of The Cross are erected on the columns surrounding the chapel.

Visit to Lithuania by Pope John Paul II, September 4, 1993.